It Gets Deeper Than Potholes

A collection of poems

Curtis "Caliber" Vanzant Jr

Caliber Van Publishing

IT GETS DEEPER THAN POTHOLES: A COLLECTION OF POEMS

Copyright © 2014 by Curtis "Caliber" Vanzant Jr. All rights reserved. Printed in the United States of America. No part of this book is not allowed to be used, reproduced, and or broadcasted in any manner whatsoever without written permission. Except for brief quotations embodied in critical articles and reviews. Spoken at events may be accepted acknowledging the author. This book can be purchased for educational use for appropriate portions thereof, business or sales promotional use.

For more information or permission address by email ccaliberdapoet@gmail.com

Cover photo by Michael Settles

Library of Congress Cataloging-in-Publication Data

Vanzant, Curtis, 1982-

It Gets Deeper Than Potholes: A Collection of Poems

ISBN- 13: 978-0692359150

ISBN- 10: 069235915X

I

Have heard many times before

To follow your heart,

I agree.

But consider the mind too.

To think of ways

For your dreams

To come true

In what you

Love to do.

Acknowledgements
Introduction

Contents

Short Poems..... 13
   My Brother 14
   What Happens 16
   Past & Present 17
   Ups & Downs 20
   My Pieces 22
   Hide & Seek 24
   When It Boils Down 25

Long Poems..... 27
   I Guess It Is What It Is 28
   A Picture Worth 1,001 37
   I Want 2B Free 49

Love Poems..... 56
   One Love 57

Grade A.................................. 73
How Do I Miss You........................ 78
One Union................................ 82
Strong Love 92

Deeper Than Just….. 99
Open & Closed Eyez...................... 100
I Remember 106
Recycled Souls.......................... 117
Gravity 127
A BIG IF 136

Something Else….. 143
In The Winter Time 144
The North Side.......................... 150
Good Morning 152
A Saturday Morning 153
Tell Me................................. 156
A Woman Scorn........................... 160

Something Different 170
   Caliber 171
   Summer 172
   Foresee It 173

Relationships 174
   Just Friends 175
   Who Gives A 181
   An Experience 190
   A Two Way Street 201

Inspiration 207
   Thanksgiving Piece 208
   The Artn Me 211

Black 222
   A Poet's Peace 223
   Ethnicity 234

Significant Days 237
   July Fourth 238
   You Only Get One 242
   Dear Valentine 250

A Fool for April 253
From Father to Son 256
Birthday Piece.................................. 270
Erotic Poetry...................................... 272
A Night of Many Nights 273
Return to Sender 282
Vacationz 293
Bilingual Love 304
For The Streets................................. 313
Broken Hearts 314
My Thoughts.................................... 320
Moment of Silence........................... 330
Choices 343
Content & Greed.............................. 351
I Am Cocaine 360
RBL 368
A Second Chance............................. 381

Hard Time 386

RB2L 391

Steel City 400

Japanese Style.. 408

Switch.. 409

Relations... 410

What I See Here 411

Road Trip 412

The Soft Side... 413

Engram 414

To All Females 421

Abused But Not Destroyed................... 423

Take Note 432

Acknowledgements

First and foremost I would like to thank our Father of all fathers for even making this possible for me. For my ups and downs that paid off in the long run in more ways than one. That blessed me with such ingenuity and tenacity in making history with my mind that meets words that not only encourage, but help motivates others. This speaks volumes that I can't stress enough.

For my parents that stuck by me. If it wasn't for the both of them again this would not be possible, to even live life for that matter.

To my grandmother and grandfather (Nellie and Ivory Perkins), I know you would be so proud of me if you both were here. I know you are here every step of the way through spirit.

To my teacher way back from Roosevelt High School literature class (Mrs. L. Tolliver), where it all started. I know you were just doing your job, but you created a spark that has been inflamed in me since then. Who would have ever thought that I would be writing a book, especially regarding poetry.

To the rest of my family, friends, and fans of the art, thanks for all your support and love. Hope I have touched every single one of you as well.

Even a few that have doubted me played a part in motivating me.

My appreciation basically goes out to everyone. Including people such as artist big or small that has inspire me.

Introduction

Although I'm a poet, words still can't express my appreciation in your purchase in this book. Every page is meaningful. Words may rhyme, but mainly it's about your life and mines. So to be as universal as I can, is the objective. In which is the reason for the name of this book, because potholes are everywhere. This book is over 15 years of work dating back from 2000-2015. You will also discover as you get further, the deeper is gets. To relate is the most important factor. I discuss a variety of issues as you will soon read and different types of poems (Acrostic, Epic, Ballad, Haiku, Lyric, Riddle, Senryu, Tanka, Free Verse, Didactic Cinquain, Horatian Ode, Diamante) plus a little erotic poetry in the mix. You can either, close your eyes and picture, or look in the mirror. This book should take you there, even if it's just for a moment. So enjoy thanks and God bless.

It Gets Deeper Than Potholes

Short Poems…..

Curtis Caliber Vanzant

My Brother

I keep smoking to avoid stress

Every day is the same

To keep the pain

Out my chest

Rest in peace my older brother

You made it to the top

Up there with the big dog

Nobody can stop

It Gets Deeper Than Potholes

A loved one dead and gone

And another mourns his death

Clueless to the day

When I breathe my last breath

Curtis Caliber

My first poem
4/20/2000

What Happens

What happens often

Is that blessings

Come in increments

Not bundles

Past & Present

To disperse in any direction

We must not forget

That we are ordinary people

Like John Legend

Taken back into time

To things that were relevant

Would you have done things different?

Think about it

Sometimes it's best to talk about it

To get it off your chest

While good things come

To those who wait
This is only determined
By ones level of faith

Believing and succeeding
Dreams are promised
Goals accomplished

Happiness comes

It Gets Deeper Than Potholes

As a gift to the present

Ups & Downs

The true meaning of life
Is learning how to live

Throughout our years
And through the vallies

To survive
Everyday is a constant step

To wake up is a blessing, but only
An introduction to new obstacles

It Gets Deeper Than Potholes

So even though we may manage

It's easier said than done
But just not the same

Caught by surprise
It doesn't necessarily have to
Thunder

Before you feel
The rain

My Pieces

I think of poetry

As a relationship

Some of my work

Are related

And outside the relationship

I have unrelated pieces

But since I'm the author

I am the father of all

It Gets Deeper Than Potholes

My babies

I feed them ears and eyes

I protect and

Fully clothe them

With copyrights

Curtis Caliber Vanzant

Hide & Seek

Majority of the time

God's gift or

Our talents

Can be found

In hobbies

It Gets Deeper Than Potholes

When It Boils Down

Religion be the lic

While gangs be like

Like politics

Republican or democrat

Red or blue

You choose

Money matters

And brain splatters

The truth is never

Handed to you

On a silver platter

Curtis Caliber Vanzant

More like under the kitchen table

If you able

It Gets Deeper Than Potholes

Long Poems…..

Curtis Caliber Vanzant

I Guess It Is What It Is

Just imagine a world without a single confused

Little boy or girl, misguided youth

Without the hype or

Without the false hope of being

Hood rich

From selling dope or doing

Whatever bad for cash

Just to eat right, see

It Gets Deeper Than Potholes

No offense but

If that's what you love to do then

That's a different story

So please don't bore me with the

I gotta get it how I live speech

While we as poets

Try to find words just to reach you

But if a man is hunger

Let alone got nothing to loose

How can you tell him

What he not going to do and

For every cause there's an effect

Just like with some of these

Elected government officials

From promoting certain videos to

Signing contracts

There's usually a catch behind that

But this is America

Home of the brave

Land of the free right

It Gets Deeper Than Potholes

According to some countries

We labeled as bullies

While pacifying others

Even though we got our own issues

To handle

So who is held accountable?

Us taxpayers?

Because if you not serving time

They coming after your pockets

Because they are gonna get theirs

Regardless

And with the national debt rising

The unemployment rate

Shouldn't be no surprising

But something to look into

I been through a few hard times

So my state of mind is a little

Different now

Because I know bad news travel fast and

It Gets Deeper Than Potholes

The media feeds off negativity so
The cycle continues

Now I'm all for my black president
But what's evident is that he's
Taken a big risk

Still hearing about hate crimes
So it's obvious that racism still
Exist

We came a long way, but we got to
Keep it moving
Maybe take up a trade or go to school and

Major in something

But see it's all about sacrifices and

Opportunity cost

Because sometimes

That what it takes to be the boss but

Whatever your legitimate hustle is

Don't mind the haters or

Professionally known as critics

Just

Think of them as……..

It Gets Deeper Than Potholes

Cheerleaders without the pom poms

Because they always got

Something to say or do

Knowing that……..

If it was the other way around

They would be saying f*** you too

So don't get it twisted

Because this not nothing new

I'm just another poet

Curtis Caliber Vanzant

Speaking…… the truth

But

I guess it is

What it is

A Picture Worth 1,001

Spoken word………..

Something that can be expressed and compressed

From more than a thousand words

Like…………pictures

The basic ingredient to a recipe

The added seasons

Are the notes, harmony and melody

Converted into music

Now whether you use it or not

What can't be forgot

Is the way it moves you

Sooths you

Calms your soul in certain situations

Even when you feel forsaken

May even get you to thinking

See this is the message I send

And as a poet I got a habit

It Gets Deeper Than Potholes

Of being outspoken…………

Now I'm working on the church

Going part but

God knows my heart

And hears from me daily

Because even the devil be trying

So hard to pursued me

Which is…………blasphemy

Curtis Caliber Vanzant

You see………..

But I'm from Gary, Indiana

Chicago's next door neighbors

So you know we not no strangers

To the street life

But despite the steel city

All I see is

Fast money, penitentiary or the grave

Call it slave work if you want

No disrespect

It Gets Deeper Than Potholes

But you can't collect a pension from dealing

Or even benefits

I mean it's just not worth it

Yes it's true

That I don't know everything nor perfect

Just invest in

A better life insurance policy

That is worth it

While life goes on because

Guess what………………

Babies still will be born

And that same ol song

Is going to be played to a

Different beat

Still trying to get through

What you thought was lost

Or the

Cause to that effect

Or why ends never met

Searching for that right one

That you haven't found yet

It Gets Deeper Than Potholes

Sometimes it's hard to

Forgive for what people did

But we can never forget

I just sit

No regrets

Trying to change some things

I can correct like

My way of thinking

My appetite or motivation

For wanting more

Curtis Caliber Vanzant

Even though doors may continue to close

So roll the dice to see what's next

Besides these………..

Up and down gas prices

And war

These wars that have caused more

Pain

Death and confusion

With little success

And no solution

It Gets Deeper Than Potholes

Corruption……………
Let's not even get on that

I guess my dad was right it's like
A jungle slash sea world out here
You got your long sharks your
Snakes, rats etc
They all plan to attack
And manipulate to kill faith
However you relate
Before you even get a chance to
Speculate so

Curtis Caliber Vanzant

What is your definition?
Of freedom though

Surrounded by this
Political, social, racial
And economical spectrum

The last thing we need is
Another lecture or speech

But the least I can do is
Speak my piece and voice my

Opinion

As long as I keep it true to myself

While my heart is still beating

Pictures

Are not painted perfect

My life is never worthless

But priceless with a purpose

I say although pictures

Are not painted perfect

Curtis Caliber Vanzant

My life is never worthless

But priceless

With a purpose

I Want 2B Free

I want to be free

Free from all the bull****

Free from the lies and deceit

They try to fill

Our conscious minds with

Who really benefits from this nation

Emancipation is a must

Temptation and devastation

Curtis Caliber Vanzant

Must cease

In order to have peace

As well as in the streets

Some wanting to change
But they in the game too deep
Treading on thin ice
Can't get the ground beneath your feet

So wake up my brother
Cause most of these cats
Are already in a permanent sleep

It Gets Deeper Than Potholes

While their families weep

Because the streets can take you under

Make you wonder like

Stevie what's next

And the war in Iraq

Has been blown way out of context

We have enough turmoil on our

Own Soil

So where do we go from here is the question?

Curtis Caliber Vanzant

Mistake made and learned

As a lesson got us counting every blessing

We need a rise a rise above all

Overcoming downfalls and pitfalls

That holds us back

Steady recovering and still

Dealing with the past that held us back

We had enough knocking on doors

For opportunity when no one

It Gets Deeper Than Potholes

Would open up

I guess that explain why we got

28 Days to celebrate

Black History Month

This is my complaint

I'm speaking for all people

Because we all supposed to be

Equal

At least treated that way

Sometimes the right way seems

Impossible

So we forced to do s*** illegal

See my story is not no different from

Yours

I refuse to be silent

But I'm gone let life take its course

Because after all

God is the source

Keep close what means the most

Find peace within yourself

Knowledge is power

Reading is fundamental

So I keep them on my shelf

For words of wisdom

And if you reading this

You will know

That life

Is what you make of it

Full of things that is not

Promised

Curtis Caliber Vanzant

Love Poems…..

It Gets Deeper Than Potholes

One Love

This

Piece symbolizes

How I truly feel

And at this particular moment

At this point in time

I come to find

That what I feel is real

I once heard that

Action speaks louder than words

Like verbs that run with adjectives

Curtis Caliber Vanzant

I can show you what I mean

And to hear your heartbeat

Next to me, well we

Produce rhythm & blues

Into our own shoes

As we engage in intimacy

Because foreplay is only the

Beginning

And as you close your eyes and

It Gets Deeper Than Potholes

Feel me

You shall receive all of me

No broken hearts just

Just broken headboards

Lord knows how much you mean to me

Because we are compatible

I like to call it

Love Avenue

And since

Curtis Caliber Vanzant

Home is where the heart is

Then let our lungs be the passages

In which we inhale and exhale

These feelings

As if

It was in the air that we

Breathe……….

Let our veins

Be the streets and lanes

That leads to those emotions

And treated

It Gets Deeper Than Potholes

As more than just

A vital organ

See what's more important

Is the time spent

With the years of us being together

Through whatever

As evidence

Because your presence

Is so heaven sent

In other words

Curtis Caliber Vanzant

This is no accident

Nor a coincidence on how we met

Therefore during these difficult

Times that we facing

You are a living blessing

Which means that your birthday

Should be a celebration

Like president Obama's

Inauguration………

So to answer your question

It Gets Deeper Than Potholes

Yes

You would mean that much to me

Describing our chemistry

As in the laws of gravity

That holds us together

By the grace of God

And if the devil was to even

Attempt

To break us up

Well, then he has one hell of a job

Not focusing on our flaws or faults

That we have

Or once had in the past with

Moving forward

At the point of no return

As being the objective

Cause if it wasn't for those failed

Relationships

Then maybe

It Gets Deeper Than Potholes

Just maybe

We wouldn't be so selective

Once again……….

If it wasn't for those failed

Relationships

Then maybe

Just maybe

We wouldn't be so selective

See unlike the movie

Curtis Caliber Vanzant

"Coming to America"

Unfortunately, I didn't meet you in Queens but

I was taught to treat you like one
I was taught to
Find that one to love and

Even on some occasions
Run your bath water

Wash your back and feet
In the bathtub
So

It Gets Deeper Than Potholes

F*** a dime piece

That would be like insulting your

Intelligence

Because that does not completely

Define your elegance

That's just a small fraction

A small portion of you

Because you would actually have

Four more qualities

With the E-quality of a

50 cent piece and

If it was up to me

Your face would be on that coin

Instead of John Kennedy's

Wanting me as your other half

Because

Together

Together we make a dollar

Any disagreements that we had

Bury that

As matter of fact

Our ongoing moments of passion

It Gets Deeper Than Potholes

And just me being with you

We should cherish that

A recollection on things

We been through

Like damn

I want to marry that

Or just following the vials of marriage

And we not even married yet

See

This may all sounds good and all

But

Curtis Caliber Vanzant

What if it doesn't work?

I mean
Will it still feel right?
If the truth hurts or
Is this just another verse?
To this piece that I wrote

My guess is just as good as yours
And considering that we not
Perfect
And only human then
We may never know

It Gets Deeper Than Potholes

But I be damn for next

If it doesn't show

So

I will make sure like

I will make sure like

My name was Al B Sure himself

While

Some shack up and tie that knot

For the wrong reasons but

That should not be the case for us

So let's just……

Take a chance based on

Curtis Caliber Vanzant

How we feel today

Because that's all we can do and
If it's best that we should breakup
Due to other issues

Then I will only remember

I will only remember

The good moments

It Gets Deeper Than Potholes
Grade A

I fell in love with her

At the age of eighteen

Different from my first

Physical love at nineteen

We met in literature class

The sensitivity was creativity of her

That made me think

And bring ideas to mind

With reason and rhyme

Curtis Caliber Vanzant

I was inspired by her realness

Of being honest

Plus she smelled good too

Like vanilla

In which I thought of ice cream

She even enjoyed the simple things

And was very observant to surroundings

Writing down my thoughts

And feelings on paper

Our best friends was the pen

That we connect to

It Gets Deeper Than Potholes

And then there was the microphone

Hitting home with words

That others can feel

And understand

But then in retrospect

When I started out

It was a blind spot

Because not a soul

Seen it coming

I get excited

When she is complete

Loving the reciting of me

Exposing her naked truth

I thought was weird

A fetish for ears

But also

Touched hearts as well

No common name like Lisa

She was the core

Like the bread to a pizza

It Gets Deeper Than Potholes

Before you add

The tasty toppings

Entertainment is her thing

But to change lives

And to stimulate

Is her forte

Her name

Is Mrs. Poetry All Day

How Do I Miss You

I miss your presence

I wish

I wish you can come back for Christmas

And was literally wrapped

As a present

I miss you like the sun

That misses the stars at night

Like being prepared to take off

And had a delayed flight

It Gets Deeper Than Potholes

Because obviously

Pictures is not good enough for me

We may not be

Completely on the same page

Or attached with titles but

At least we were in the same book

And that is

What counted the most

I rather boast about the good

Rather than complain over stuff so little

You can't

See the reason behind it

Because we were

No other than significant

But that was back then

And I still miss you

Your company was my home

Unfortunately

More than likely

You don't realize that

Until it's gone………..

Or taken

To move forward

It Gets Deeper Than Potholes

Is my only

Option

You make me want to

Give my heart up for adoption

Like the rest

That gives up

On

Love

Curtis Caliber Vanzant

One Union

I can actually say that I

Found my soul mate

Investing and anticipating on happiness

Out of love and commitment

Family be the result of this equation

Without persuasion

We already been

Following the vials

For a while now

It Gets Deeper Than Potholes

Why not tie the not

To make it official

No more

Throwing in the towel

Or time outs

When blowing the whistle

Let's continue

The journey as one union

Starting from day one

Let's be like those Romans

Curtis Caliber Vanzant

With our loyalty

Just as rich as royalty

While others

Just make trade offs

Look at us

We at it again

Again and again

As we make love

To our best friends

Which is you and me

Like Beyoncé's

Drunken Love

We both get a buzz off each other

As if

We were up all night

Wine tasting until

We got wasted

Putting aside

The things that we are

Normally faced with

Because at this very moment

That's all that matters

Curtis Caliber Vanzant

At first as kids

You was my girlfriend

We grew up

Grown and sexy

That's when

You became my lady

Now my wife

Vice versa

With the forever promise

It Gets Deeper Than Potholes

That a ring holds

Should bring us closer

Because we

Got history

Exactly where we left

Childish games

And breaking up at

Whether or not

We go way back

I gladly take pride

In being

Your husband

Call me

Mr. Right's younger brother

No better yet

Call me his cousin

Embracing my flaws

And I just found out

What page you on?

The last paragraph of 10

It Gets Deeper Than Potholes

But what's ironic

Is when I proposed that day

I was at the beginning

Of page 11

An abundance of love

To be oneness

Like limbs I would care for

So therefore you would

Be a part of me like

Poetry

And unlike "Vacationz"

You know

It's permanent

Even though

I'm sometimes skeptical

About certain things

Nevertheless

I believe that

I made the right move

So I say to you

In holy matrimony

It Gets Deeper Than Potholes

I do

Curtis Caliber Vanzant

Strong Love

I guess I was

Her type of caliber

And for me

She was more than

Eye candy

But a tourist attraction

In my mind

That had me thinking

Of at least five positions

It Gets Deeper Than Potholes

After she was no longer

A guest in my house

I started to wonder

How would she be as my spouse?

Because this was that

Strong love

Unconditional like above

No temps allowed

That made me appreciate

What I been through

Up into now

If both hands were broken

She would pick my boogers

With her own fingers

How do I know?

Because she said so

Even likes it better

When I do it

To her slow

It Gets Deeper Than Potholes

Beyond the same page

More like the same heart beat

Synchronized breathing

As we sleep

Plus she supports

And loves what I do

As if she was the stage

And I was the performer

Behind closed doors

Curtis Caliber Vanzant

Tasting ingredients was extra

The feeling

Was mutual

Scary but tolerable

And stronger than

The first year

A deal breaker unlike most

So why messed that up

Good sex

Like her cooking

It Gets Deeper Than Potholes

Some things in common

It's been over a year separated

And we still can hold a

Conversation

Taking turns with the kids

Through the courts

Even though

They may wish for more

We don't conflict but compromise

Respect

With a bond that only

Curtis Caliber Vanzant

Death can take

Only physically

A strong love

That remains

From within

It Gets Deeper Than Potholes

Deeper Than Just…..

Curtis Caliber Vanzant

Open & Closed Eyez

I open my eyes, what do I see

A young mother with tears in her eyes

She's so happy

I finally unfold up out the wound

And unaware of how this world

Was doomed

I cry also

Cold cause I needed warmth

Luv in which I needed some

It Gets Deeper Than Potholes

Problems cause I haven't seen none

Up into now

My heart slowly beats and

Evil by myself

I can't defeat

My temperature drops

And once again

I am cold

Not because I needed warmth

But because God said

That it was time to go

And I quietly

Closed my eyes

Not knowing what's in store in the after life

Without body, my soul is breathless

And left with no conscience

And no feeling

But if I still had a mind

I would think

Of the tangible and some of the

Intangible things

That I left behind

It Gets Deeper Than Potholes

So if you shall remorse then do so

In tears of joy

To celebrate in my demise

Because I have risen to a better place

Above man

Above laws and society that

Tries to put us in

Invisible handcuffs

Above enemies even though

I was told to love and pray for them too

Curtis Caliber Vanzant

Free from the sins of man

I mean real freedom

See I was exposed to these issues

And now I'm just as simple as a

Breeze in the air

Watching over you

For a change

Because I care

And touching you with my words

Find me in the heavens

With my creator

My savior

My friend

Untouchable to the devil

So in other words

God wins

Again

Curtis Caliber Vanzant

I Remember

I remember

I remember when we

Was younger

Living in the same city

But from different hoods

Even claimed different gangs

Cause we could

You was in it deeper than

I ever was

It Gets Deeper Than Potholes

But you was my blood

Plus I loved you no matter what

Because that's how we rolled

Despite dealing with

The dice that was already rolled

While I was into the arts

You played biddy

When Bad Boy records

Was on the rise

And it was Puffy

Curtis Caliber Vanzant

Before it was Diddy

You even had a

Distinctive laugh

Like Eddie Murphy

But I missed that

Especially

The time

When we lived in MN

And talked about going back

Unfortunately

Your return to Gary

It Gets Deeper Than Potholes

Is when things got harder

If it wasn't for you

I wouldn't of knew

What some of these

Other dudes go through

Personally

So I prayed for your mercy

And instead of getting answered

It got switched in the process

As an example

Curtis Caliber Vanzant

With a dead end sign

At the end of the road

You was somewhat cautious thou

Only for a short minute

After baby boy was born

Then father died

Taking more risks

Than a little bit

Trying to make ends meet

Everything was temporary

That was good

It Gets Deeper Than Potholes

Even college

On and off between gigs

With no leads

Now you hustling again

In this situation

Money gets impossible to hold

In your hand

Like water

You can be respected

But the streets

Still don't care

Who you are

I even remember when you named me

Godfather

I was proud

But somehow

That really wasn't allowed

I tried to be in his life

But like all things regarding in

Building a relationship

It Gets Deeper Than Potholes

It's a two way street

We live and

We learn

I just couldn't grasp

The understanding of that

One hundred

And eighty degree turn

Which is what I did

Once I walked up

To you laying in that casket

They say to celebrate

Of another's passing

But I was grieving

And didn't want to be bothered

For a few days

Thinking about it

Like I just

Got the bad news yesterday

Who would have ever predicted

That you would have only 23 years

To live

But God

It Gets Deeper Than Potholes

Almost two months away

From your birthday

Anyway

Needless to say

Life goes on

But I remember

I remember

The memory of you

Still lives on

Curtis Caliber Vanzant

Like these spoken words

That I jot down on paper

So no goodbyes

I will just

See you later

So see you later

It Gets Deeper Than Potholes
Recycled Souls

What if an individual

Can have such an impact on the World

And other people

Whether it was good or bad

That their soul can be recycled

Understanding that this is Reincarnation

Transformed in another or living Form

Beyond scientific explanations

That some say

Doesn't exist

Curtis Caliber Vanzant

Remembering past lives

As evidence

Ever since off springs
Came with new beginnings
In which poses the question

What is the true definition?
Of being born again

Living in sin
But still forgiven
An often

It Gets Deeper Than Potholes

In disbelief and criticize what

Sounds strange or don't make

Sense to us

Instead of thinking outside the box

As if you were

Stuck between a rock

And a hard place

You don't have faith

Then you wouldn't know the God

That I know

Curtis Caliber Vanzant

In the first place

Plus you say

This is not your first case but

It just maybe your last

I know cats that lived fast

And died fast

All for that cash

From GI to Chicago

Where violence disperses

Like a bad rash

But see

It Gets Deeper Than Potholes

I'm open minded

If you research long enough

You shall find it

Recycled souls in families

That is nothing like commodities

Or

Aluminum cans

That you take to a place

To get melted down and reused

More like guardian angels

Curtis Caliber Vanzant

Or people that come into your lives

And you don't know why

The ones that claim

They haven't been the same

From the time when

John and Jane Doe died

I speak for you

Let my words

Hit you like alcohol

To an open wound

And heal you

Because the

It Gets Deeper Than Potholes

The truth hurts

Even though sometimes we prefer

Not to hear it

And what's relevant is not visible

That it lies from within one's

Spirit

Disguised in

Friends, business or pleasure

These recycled souls are tricky

These recycled souls

Can even come in bad weather

Or when you least expected

That way we are

Never neglected

But selected by delegation

Opposite from

Jesus's resurrection

So watch

Watch as it unfolds

Like a young man

With an old soul

That had me thinking that

It Gets Deeper Than Potholes

Somehow, somewhere

In another dimension

On judgment day

When it was mentioned

To return

For a purpose

Or without any intentions

Then again

I could be right or wrong but

I'm only stating my opinion

Curtis Caliber Vanzant

As ironic as this may sound

I just might be one of those

Recycled souls

It Gets Deeper Than Potholes
Gravity

According to

The similarity in Einstein's theory

And Newton's

Laws of Gravity

It states that two bodies or matter

Attract each other

By force

Of course

I'm talking about things falling but

Much more complex than that

A disconnect of self-control

Curtis Caliber Vanzant

A gravitational pull

That draws you in

Like a magnet

The same reason why

Two people

May fall

For each other

<u>Energy, distance and mass</u>

But the formula

Is already complicated enough

For me to explain

So why ask

It Gets Deeper Than Potholes

How is it possible

That it holds

Between events

That you assume is a coincidence

In which you both stand

Whether it was that lifestyle

Chasing that green

That dream that

Same good feeling

Or just

A moment of happiness

That you haven't had

In a long while

Now that's a broad subject

Physics at its best

Because what goes up

Well

You know the rest

And the reverse effect

Depends on the acceleration that

Forces the object or objects

It Gets Deeper Than Potholes

To still travel

In a downward spiral

But a different direction

Now

You can earn love and trust

Unless it's given up at first

To keep

For your king or queen

You would do anything

For a God

Curtis Caliber Vanzant

Or whatever it is you believe

You bow down to his feet

To come close

Or to push away from

Due to certain circumstances

That destroys

Second chances

Crossing over that thin line

With a heart

On the verge

Of being

It Gets Deeper Than Potholes

Flat lined

Because for whatever reason

It has been broken

And to repair

Make take a lifetime

Like a wound

Without a scab

Left open

Is it fixable?

Oh yeah, it's possible

If all of what I just said

Sounds logical

And I was only talking about

Energy and distance

The mass is the weight

When situations get heavy

And the burden that it carries

Can bring

You

Down

Unless you change its path

In the process

Basically

It Gets Deeper Than Potholes

It's all about

Falling

Imagine a heart

Still beating

But covered

In bloody bandages

Because some of us

Have fallen

Out of love

Curtis Caliber Vanzant

A BIG IF

If I was a star then
She would be my moon

If Jesus is coming back
Then he shall return soon
Around noon

But actually within us
As if he was our conscious
If there wasn't a such thing
As death

It Gets Deeper Than Potholes

And Adam never ate that fruit

Would the world be over crowded?

Events that happen

To repeat a cycle

What if souls really were recycled?

And in the plan

Or no hate

Just love

This would be the promise land

Like heaven

Curtis Caliber Vanzant

On earth

And not above

If there were no justice

Just

Us

Even though that does happen

Often anyway

If all can think

For themselves

Instead of being persuaded

If people did treat others

It Gets Deeper Than Potholes

The way they wanted to be treated

Innocent until proven guilty

If republicans

Wasn't so damn filthy

America

The corporation

Turned upside down in rotation

With it being

Hot up north

And cold

Curtis Caliber Vanzant

Like winter chills

In the south

No unfed mouths

Deadbeats or

Women scorned

If unborn babies

Were actually given a choice

To be born

If the person you rejected

Convicted

Ignored or overlooked

It Gets Deeper Than Potholes

Was actually telling the truth

If today

Was your last

To speak to a loved one

Before they past

A Big If

Like a change

That doesn't even exist

What if

Curtis Caliber Vanzant

What if

I wasn't a poet

I probably wouldn't be able to

Tell it to you

Like this

It Gets Deeper Than Potholes

Something Else…..

Curtis Caliber Vanzant

In The Winter Time

It's officially winter now

Not only cold

But the snow sticks to the ground

I sit and ponder about

Rain with thunder

Being like a precursor of it

Snow is quiet when it comes down

No warnings and no sound

It Gets Deeper Than Potholes

In the winter time

It seems like the days go by

A little slower than usual

Because more time is spent indoors

For some

And for others

This is the best season

With every reason to go out

In the winter time

I often think of the summer time

And can't wait for its arrival

Curtis Caliber Vanzant

Watching movies

Staying warm

Just might

Write a piece about civilization

Racial profiling

Or the way racism still exists

But more mentally

What about the dying of our youth

The loss of our troops

The single mothers

We need more fathers

It Gets Deeper Than Potholes

Instead of baby daddies

Or the way AIDS spread

Like it's a common cold now in

Days

Or to just write a piece

About the winter time

The time where you

Spend more dollars

And putting in hours

Just before

The holidays

With plenty of things

To be thankful for

In the winter time

A lot of babies are conceived

Lovers rekindle their flames

The heat of the moment is

Pleasurable

And quality time is well

Appreciated

These are some of the things

It Gets Deeper Than Potholes

That I think about when

I think of the winter time

Because in the winter time

A one of a kind

Capricorn

Was born

Curtis Caliber Vanzant

The North Side

Cold, but quiet

Not violent

But silent

A mixture of

All kinds there

Diversity versus opportunity

With roads of hills

And still, I would

Like to go there again

It Gets Deeper Than Potholes

The state of Twin Cities

A pair

I rather go in the summer
Because in the winter
Snow is everywhere
Above just a foot

Curtis Caliber Vanzant

Good Morning

The first blessing

Is waking up

And to tackle new obstacles

Or

To overcome

The ones

That stopped you yesterday

It Gets Deeper Than Potholes
A Saturday Morning

8'oclock Saturday morning

The forecast say

"It's going to be 80 degrees today"

And birds are chirping out my window

I really don't plan things

Except for

Special occasions and deadlines

So what I was going to do

Was all on the mood

Curtis Caliber Vanzant

The proper outfit

Has been officially decided

And laid out on the bed

A shower first and then breakfast

With grits, potatoes, 2 eggs, and

Three bacons

And some milk to drink

Everything was done

Unfortunately, I had a long

Friday night

It Gets Deeper Than Potholes

So my head was aching

It was just after eleven

The fact that

I have awaken

Was the reason

It was

A good morning

Curtis Caliber Vanzant

Tell Me

What are your fears?

What are your dislikes?

What is the chance?

That you might leave

Because you think that

One is not considering your feelings

Throwing temper tantrums

It Gets Deeper Than Potholes

While saying

Screw you

As the anthem

See when you branch off

To date someone new

He or she only hears your story

In which can be

Freely fabricated

You give your girls advice

On how to keep a man

But you can't keep this one

You miss one

Spending the rest of your life

Or just a few years

Looking for a replacement

And rebounds

So how can a person

Treat you totally the same

It's either

Better

Or worse

It Gets Deeper Than Potholes

Your opinion

My experience

And at what point

Does this poem end?

With you

Curtis Caliber Vanzant

A Woman Scorn

She was a good woman at first

Gone bad

I mean she gave this dude

All she had

That was priceless

Even bought him some nice shit

And in return

All he gave her was d***

It Gets Deeper Than Potholes

She believed she was in love

And he would not only love

But lust for her

Like he did others

She was confused

And didn't know what to do

Becoming tired of being faithful

She did her thing

While he

Ran the streets

Curtis Caliber Vanzant

Until she started to fill nauseous

Weak and throwing up

A pregnancy test

Was the next action

She been pregnant

For one month

Then decided

To get an abortion

But changed her mind

Once she got there

It Gets Deeper Than Potholes

Do you see where?

I'm going with this

I don't think so…….

Because this story gets

Deeper than potholes

Covered by melted snow

And rain water

The baby was born

A boy with a head full of hair

The father

Unknown

Is when she

Realized that she

Had to do everything

On her own

She said she had enough

Of it

An adoption

I guess

Was the best option

That she came up with

It Gets Deeper Than Potholes

This is reality

Which means

There are no commercials in

Between

Not even a movie

But she began

To depend on

Good times

With multiple partners

As her escape goat

Not knowing what's about to

Take place

She's curious

Plus she

Haven't been

Going to her

Regular check ups

Since she gave

The baby up

She wanted to get tested for

Everything

It Gets Deeper Than Potholes

And I mean everything

Unfortunately

There was good news

And bad news

The test results

Came back negative

For the majority of STD's

Even herpes

But positive for HIV

Furious

Curtis Caliber Vanzant

But somehow kept her cool

Revengeful and

Heartless

She uses

Her good looks and assets

To lure them in

Blaming all men

As if she

Was completely innocent

And wanted to get even

A woman scorned

It Gets Deeper Than Potholes

Like a short story

In poetry form

More like

The Jezebels of our time

I hope you got the point

That I was trying to make

Practice safe

And wrap

It up

Curtis Caliber Vanzant

Something Different…..

Caliber

A partiCular person that is

Opposite of whAt is usual

Not always typicaL

Irreplaceable

Born to be

SomEwhat unorthodox

Unpopular to the majoRity but

Unique

Curtis Caliber Vanzant

Summer

Summer

Fun, hot

Enticing, relaxing, exploring

A season to enjoy

Heat

Foresee It

Our

Imperfections allows us

To determine the destination from

Where we came from to

Where we are going

By the end

Of X

(Diamante)

Curtis Caliber Vanzant

Relationships…..

Just Friends

All of that time together

And it came to this

You and me separated over some bull****

But I had to quit

I had to throw in the towel

Because it was either me or him

I eliminated myself

For the simple fact that

I can do bad all by myself

Curtis Caliber Vanzant

You became bad for my health

Like cigarettes

But I would never forget

How it was when we first met

It was all good back then

Even in the summer time

Know you know

How the summer time get

You kept my attention

And not to mention the TLC

That was given, I appreciated it

It Gets Deeper Than Potholes

The time we spent

The laughs we had

Me being around your son

Like I was his Dad

So it wasn't easy

The relationship took a toll on me

And I know you had feelings for

Me

Maybe it's just not meant to be

Maybe it is good for us to know of

Each other

Not be together

Whether we like it or not

Not knowing how long it would

Last

The past is now behind us

Left with only one solution

And that's to move on

Somewhat like an emotional relief

Hope dude is everything

He claim or

What you think he is to be

It Gets Deeper Than Potholes

Because if you can't choose me

Or confused and can't make

A chose at all

Then obviously, you not the one

For me

Yeah, we still cool though

But I refuse to be somebody's fool though

So my answer to your question

Where do we go from here?

I guess I separate ways

Curtis Caliber Vanzant

Like people say

All things must come to an end

And I think we should do the same

But I want to remain

Just friends

It Gets Deeper Than Potholes

Who Gives A

Now I don't mean to sound cold or

Bold

I just rather be honest, no game

Running or strings attached

Not saying you not a good catch

I mean

We might even be a match

But I'm on auto pilot

Better yet cruise controlling

Curtis Caliber Vanzant

So there is no need to exceed to

Greater expectations

And what the hell is an

Open relationship anyway

The only difference is

One extra word too many

To describe your status

Like saying

I like or

I love you

I want you as

It Gets Deeper Than Potholes

My main boo

Although I want to screw other

People

Which means you can't have

All of this

You better off being promiscuous

Why even bother telling lies

Just to tell another

Cause I want you as my

Significant other

Too much s*** to remember

To cover

Curtis Caliber Vanzant

I figger

If I was to be rude or

Lightly obnoxious

Then why not now

Eliminating any shocking surprises

That would lead to confusion

And too late reactions

Cause you so called

Blinded by your love for me

When I wore my heart on my sleeve

It Gets Deeper Than Potholes

Only a few showed their love for me

So welcome

Welcome to REALITY

In other words

I don't want you wasting time

Putting your eggs all in one basket

Trying so hard to believe that

What me and you got is magic

Unless you can convinced me

Otherwise

Because love hurts like a paper cut

Plus

I took enough chances

Not saying it doesn't exist

I'm just so tired of bull****

See

You may have your men stories

In which for me

Is the total opposite

Even though we attract because of it

What we got in common is what

Started this

It Gets Deeper Than Potholes

But regardless

Who gives a damn about your

Feelings

I told you I'm single

It's not all about me wanting to mingle

Because as far as good sex goes

That has potential

To be mutual

And no I'm not using you

How about this

Let's tell

A truth for a truth

To avoid disputes and accusations

It's not that I don't care

It's just not fair

To take it there

Because once we go further

Then here comes the arguments

Where things between us get sour

Instead of working it out

I get the weak excuse of

It Gets Deeper Than Potholes

I'm so busy

Or the silent treatment of a coward

Maybe we

We moved too fast based on lust

And in order to fix this

We should

Grow towards a more robust

Friendship

But until then

Who gives a damn

Curtis Caliber Vanzant

An Experience

She called me

She called me

And asked me

Was it a full moon that night?

Cause I made love to her

For the first time like

Like the last time endlessly

As if

It Gets Deeper Than Potholes

I was going away

The next day

To go fight

For my country

So we tried role playing

And pretended to be strangers

Like we just met all over again

Only this time

This time my name was Mustafa

From Africa

And her name was Cattleya

Curtis Caliber Vanzant

Queen of all flowers

From Columbia

But don't let the

Soft spoken voice fool you

I'm mean

She was cool too

With the sexiest lips

That can talk as much s*** as I do

Instead of flee

We were compatible

It Gets Deeper Than Potholes

She make a brother

Want to get down on one knee

And say I do

See I believed that

We made R&B

While she

Was the rhythm to my heart beat

I was her blues

The true color of blood

Before it hits air particles

Holding a chemical bond

Curtis Caliber Vanzant

Like molecules and

Family oriented

Like the Hustables

I just hate starting over with the

New

Looking for something

In someone that's genuine

And reciprocal

If I only knew

That she was on games

I thought I was the poet

It Gets Deeper Than Potholes

How in the hell

Did I get to be April's fool

Didn't care for make-up or lipstick

Natural beauty was her best feature

Since size does matter

To an extent

She had no problem

With my long distance either

But somewhere between the lines of

Happiness and trust

Is where we lost touch

Disagreements turned into

Arguments

And that's when she became

Full of it

So for potential candidates

Regarding relationships

Tell me

What really is appropriate?

Bringing roses to your

Garden of Eden

Or back and forth

For no apparent reason

For all I know

You could be one of those season folk

With plenty of mood swings

In order to cope

My ultimatum would be

To stay or go

No regrets on knowing you

But in this case

It was my mistake in

Trying to date you in

The first place

So to extend an invitation

To be friends is all I offer

An experience is all it cost us

We only live once

My pops say

You can never be too cautious in

Taking chances on a daily

I can careless about a Valentine

It Gets Deeper Than Potholes

I rather have her as mine

All the time

Remembering love again

And how we use to

Dirty dance to pleasure

In the process

She even had me

Speaking in español

Like te amo……….

Cause we both was biology

Intertwined with chemistry

Curtis Caliber Vanzant

And the rest

Well the rest was history

A Two Way Street

What is it that you want?

Attention
Unlike the men you dated
That you been missing
Because rejection is hardly
Accepted

Or am I just a replacement
A continuance act of love, lust
Financial gain

Or just stability

For a connection to exceed the

Greed

That fills the need

Of wanting more

Am I potential?

Or just an open door

Either time wasted or

Time invested

Lies can roam free

While the truth

It Gets Deeper Than Potholes

Gets well rested

Instead of thinking like a man

Do you as a woman

Hope you are not too blind to see

That this

Is a two way street

That involves effort between

The both of us

No chase

Curtis Caliber Vanzant

I rather you run this race

Beside me

Maybe start a family

But in order for that to happen

We have to be on the same page

My boo

I'm just saying

If I'm on seven

How you still on page two

The love

It Gets Deeper Than Potholes

That we share

Must be reciprocal

Otherwise I'm out

Like a game of poker

I mean

I don't ask for much

So tell me

What more can a man?

Ask for

But before we

Officially meet

Curtis Caliber Vanzant

Just to let you know

That this

Is a two way street

It Gets Deeper Than Potholes

Inspiration…..

Curtis Caliber Vanzant

Thanksgiving Piece

For the body that borrow

I am blessed to see tomorrow

Knowing my fate rest in his hands

And through trials and tribulations

Thanksgiving is like a lifetime holiday

So thanks for giving me the opportunity

To survive another 365

It Gets Deeper Than Potholes

Understanding the logical behind

Overcoming obstacles

Because of you

All things are possible

And greatly appreciated

While manifested within me

My heart pumps the security

Of the blood of Christ

Without thinking twice about

What I would live and die for

Curtis Caliber Vanzant

Not a perfect one

But I'm a somewhat humble one

Forgiven for our sins by

God's only son

So what I been through

I'm truly thankful

For what I have become

It Gets Deeper Than Potholes

The Artn Me

Curtis Caliber

Just like a thesis to an essay

My name should explain it all
In more than two sentences
Until the day I reach my final fall

But unlike such papers
A statement is just not good
Enough

I must discuss a variety of issues

And things from dreams to reality

In terms of conformity and

Individuality

As in Abraham Maslow's

Hierarchy theory

Poetry in motion

In a heart beat

Like

Like the spinning of a cd

And the scratches be the internal

And external

Bodily injuries

It Gets Deeper Than Potholes

A philosophy on life

And what it endures

The comparison

A painter that paints pictures

A reflection on what

He or she

Sees or feels

Attention to detail in their works

To perfection

They tend to bring out emotion

In the viewer

Curtis Caliber Vanzant

Only verbally

A spoken word is deep

As in below sea level

Observant to surroundings

Mentally stimulating the mind

Sometimes helping you

Cope with hard times

Considered as food for thought

History

Even recognizing God's glory

It Gets Deeper Than Potholes

Outspoken

Revealing truth

Exposing self

On how love came, stayed

And left

It's

Whatever you want it to be

Painted into words

That may have meaning

But no power unless

Someone in listening or reading

Curtis Caliber Vanzant

Perhaps

Maybe affecting

The one who wrote it

Just as it may do

To the one who painted it

And that's when

It becomes more than

Entertainment

To an audience

It Gets Deeper Than Potholes

Expressions with emphasis

Creativity

Mostly likely found in those

With introverted personalities

All this and more

A philosophy on life

And what it endures

At first

It was just a hobby for me

Curtis Caliber Vanzant

Remembering

How it all started

In literature class

Is when I noticed

Because I use to just like her

Three years later

I wifed her

But it was always a piece of me

Like my feet

That keeps me

Moving forward in this life

My words is nice

It Gets Deeper Than Potholes

And God's timing

Is precise

Ever since

I was born

In that winter storm

Found

While some remain lost

In which

I believe he speaks

Through us and others

Of the same caliber

To get his point across +

Curtis Caliber Vanzant

So if I shall go

Then remember me

By my first love

Embrace hugs

Shake hands

Instead of mean mugs

Face your problems

And try solving them

Instead of

Sweeping them

Under the rug

It Gets Deeper Than Potholes

Once again

This is just a piece of me

So welcome

To the art

Of poetry

Curtis Caliber Vanzant

Black…..

It Gets Deeper Than Potholes
A Poet's Peace

If I was a Libra

If I was born a Libra

I probably would have

Got a tattoo

With the sign of a scale

Even though my good

Outweighs my bad I've had

My share of downfalls

But I see

I don't count them

I count me blessings

And among life lessons

Since God is not done with me

I can at least look forward to

Waking up

No guarantees but

Unfortunately, I have no wood to

Knock on

My hands together

So I pray for strength to carry on

Because we all know

That the devil can be just as busy

As God is

It even says in the bible

It Gets Deeper Than Potholes

To be aware of false profits

And ungodliness

Although I'm not perfect

That's why I express myself

Within the words I write instead of preach

Because to me

A poet's piece is a

Poet's peace

I'm more like

I'm more like

Your modern day Langston Hughes

Curtis Caliber Vanzant

With different issues than the

Days of the Harlem Renaissance

And the past of slavery

Believe me

I come from a big family tree

And 80's baby

Where it used to be

More hate crimes before my time

Than my generation and after me

Of genocide

Some people say

It Gets Deeper Than Potholes

"Won't you just stay black and die"

Like that's my only purpose

I guess I felt poetry was worth it

While I try to reach the ears of those

Who never even heard this

So

I spit verses

And let the names of black leaders

That died for a cause

Ring bells and

Curtis Caliber Vanzant

Be the echoes

Followed by

The reason of how we got to this point

In the first place

Meanwhile for centuries

The memory is studied

Televised

And embedded in our minds that we

Try so hard to erase

We went from getting whipped

To driving nice whips and

It Gets Deeper Than Potholes

Hello masa

To becoming managers

All professions of practice

CEO's

Even poets

That produce shows

While a few just replaced their

Shackles

For long chains to swang

Which made me realize that

Curtis Caliber Vanzant

I got something in common

With that homeless man that begs

For change

Because we as a minority we

May ask

For the same thing

Money, power, respect

Or to be recognized

And if not all four

Then this

It Gets Deeper Than Potholes

Is just a small list

Of what a person will live

And die for

It cost to be rich

And it cost to be poor

Knowing that man's everyday plan

Is that

If you have goals and credentials

Is not

To fall

Off course

Curtis Caliber Vanzant

Therefore we

Constantly tested

With trust invested

In something greater than us

While some may earn and some may take

But

No matter how much you make

Living for tomorrow

The walks of life on earth

Was only borrowed

It Gets Deeper Than Potholes

It was never bought

A revolving evolution
With an endless conclusion
This is my elucidation

Of a poet's peace

Curtis Caliber Vanzant

Ethnicity

Black beauty defines us

To struggle but to be strong

And a long way from giving up

In that same relation

One of God's greatest creations

The way we, manage to maintain

Handling things

Like an angel without wings

It Gets Deeper Than Potholes

With nothing but the blood of Christ

Bleeding through our veins

Unfortunately, mistakes our made

And hard lessons are learned

With only one concern....

To survive

Treated like the lowest of the low

Before our time

Now we respected

But sometimes disrespected

Curtis Caliber Vanzant

By our own kind

In which I have witness this

Although racism still exist

I pray to God and

Hope that he understands this

It Gets Deeper Than Potholes

Significant Days…..

Curtis Caliber Vanzant

July Fourth

I can hear those bottle rockets

Roman Candles

And all

Popping off now

There is no Big Bang Theory

On the fourth

For this

Is the day

Of the United States Independence

It Gets Deeper Than Potholes

Contrary to popular belief

I beg to differ

But I'm all for

The fireworks

As we celebrate

Our own independence

Of some kind

Within ourselves

Curtis Caliber Vanzant

To help build

That depends

On your level of tenacity

Because honestly

I think of change

Including moments whether

Far or near

Thinking of

What I did the last year

When I look up

To see sparks fly

That lights up the night's sky

A night for romance

Where families get together

To cover as well

The cookout

My question

From me to you

Where is the barbeque at?

Curtis Caliber Vanzant

You Only Get One

Many are missed, some are just

Misfit

Mothers have been around

Since the beginning of time

The primary carrier who can

Spread love

Through the whole area

Unconditionally, it was meant to

Be

It Gets Deeper Than Potholes

Conceived within those wounds

With a voice so sweet

Kicking her belly I can't wait to

Meet

A child is finally born

But this is no promise land and

No man can be

More supportive than your mama can

Emotionally

And in the words of the

Late great James Brown

Curtis Caliber Vanzant

It's a man's world

But mothers make the world go

Around

Never stopping humanity
The love for my mother
Is one thing I will take
To the grave with me because
You only get one

And to be mama's only son

It Gets Deeper Than Potholes

Raising us back then

I'll never forget where I came from

Even as a poet

Words can't express enough

My appreciation for her not having

That abortion

But I will always remember

"I brought you in this world and

I can take you out"

Without a shadow of a doubt

For a minute

I believed that

This piece was made

To give positive feedback to those

Especially the ones that have to

Play

The father's role

With goals that get held back

While still putting food on the

Table

It Gets Deeper Than Potholes

I mean we struggle, but we was

Able

And some stuff just wasn't fair

So thank God for welfare

My childhood was steady

I was an active little boy

But mama made sure

The home cook meals was ready

The list goes on and on

And if I could sing I would sing a

Song

Knowing that

The respect that I do have

For some females came from home

Now

I might not have been planned in

Yours eyes

But according to God

He said I was no mistake

So putting up

It Gets Deeper Than Potholes

With some of the dust that

Me and my sister

I kicked up

I just want to say thanks

Happy Mother's Day

Curtis Caliber Vanzant

Dear Valentine

Many celebrate

While others can careless

But on this day the upmost

Affection

For another is stressed

Now I know this is not nothing but

A friendship

Type of love

It Gets Deeper Than Potholes

I'm just letting you know

I value that

And wouldn't take back

Nor regret for one sec

See cards sometimes don't exactly

Express

How I feel

So I just

Write what is real

Hoping you understand my emotion

Curtis Caliber Vanzant

Nothing more, nothing less

Natural beauty at its best

And knowing that

Being friends was always

The first step

HAPPY VALENTINE'S DAY

A Fool for April

Now I won't say I loved

Every woman

I came across

And I'm sure they can say

The same

But I had serious feelings for her

She was also the daughter

Of a preacher

In which I heard

Curtis Caliber Vanzant

To be careful

I got to admit

She was pretty slick

Especially when she mixed

Truth with deception

Hoping I wouldn't tell

The difference

I was all ears

And even provided a Kleenex

For her crocodile tears

It Gets Deeper Than Potholes

About how men treated her

In her past life

That I had nothing to do with

Or deserve

So much for getting hitched

I guess payback really is a bitch

Excuse my language

I was just a fool

A fool

For April

Curtis Caliber Vanzant

From Father to Son
(A conversation between me, Dad, and God)

"Son, times have changed since

I was coming up in the past

It may not have been

Effective enough but

We made do

With what we had

Which was all we needed

Everything now is all convenient

I'm old-fashion so

Some things I wish was repeated

It Gets Deeper Than Potholes

There really was no medicine

With multiple side effects
Nor pain killers to block pain
When I was a kid
Just plain old
Home remedies
From your granny
Between
My generation and yours
Holds a big discrepancy
Because you'll depend
On more than just necessities"
Please remind me, Dad

Curtis Caliber Vanzant

Elaborate on how it used to be

He looks at me

Up and down and says

"You just don't know how good

You got it

It will be

Foolish of me to say

You forgot it

Cause according to the music

And news I notice

Is that

We use to put up our dukes to fight

Yawl like to pull out guns

It Gets Deeper Than Potholes

To shoot, right

Then the audacity

To degrade women tremendously

As if

Chivalry never existed son

Like a gentleman was just

A walking corpse

From the cradle

To the coffin

Living life in a rush

The exchange of self

For wealth

But life

Curtis Caliber Vanzant

Life is like fishing"

I said, Dad

You could have

Used another example

Because for one

I'm allergic

Plus I think fishing

Is boring

"That's because you missing

My point son

You must have patience

I'm sure God agrees

As you can see

It Gets Deeper Than Potholes

Your blessings

Don't often come on your watch

Now does it"

I said, Dad

You right

Because even when I try

With all my mite

I might not get back

What I put in

In return

So I ask God

What should I do?

He said

"My son

Don't get discourage

Keep exercising

Your gift

I bestowed upon you

Let me handle

The rest

I address prayers

Not complaints

So be blessed"

And there goes my dad

Reminiscing again

"The biggest change was technology

It Gets Deeper Than Potholes

I even remember

When there was a time

Where you only needed

A high school diploma

Or GED

Now they want

Some experience

And a college degree

Or to assume

Was no room

In the mind

For being optimistic and

Joining the military

Curtis Caliber Vanzant

Was the next best legal alternative

With the greatest risk"

I say, wow

I guess what gets better with age

Is wisdom

It's just that

You can't shake off bad habits

Or hardship that easy

In order to overcome

But Dad you was lucky

A retiree that came in

With no high school diploma

"No luck son

But fortunate

It Gets Deeper Than Potholes

Including you

And your sister

Born outside of wedlock

Don't stop anything

Especially when you

Look at the number of abortions

And fatherless families

That has been a major impact

For decades

Some things change

Like state laws

While other issues remain the same

Like love for instance"

What about love Dad

"Try not to abuse it

Because some may

Use the term loosely

Only for their benefit

To the point that

It becomes useless

See I was raised in those villages

In which you'll call communities

From the south to city

Where

I had my share of fun

Flaws and mistakes

It Gets Deeper Than Potholes

That took longer to learn from

Then the time it takes

To make them

And still

No regrets

But my heart has always been

Family"

"But that was back then

That was back when son

I met your mom in 71

Your sister came in 74

A couple

Of miscarriages later

We had you in 82

When you both

Could have been

One of those two

In other words

You are here for something

So appreciate

Some of what

You go through

Because that's part of

What shapes you

Into the man you are today

No matter

How old you get"

"As far as life

To add any more significance or value

Is also up to you

And when opportunity does knock

Make sure you are

Awake"

Curtis Caliber Vanzant

Birthday Piece

See over the years of ups and downs

I had my fair share

So I try to prepare even though

My predictions are never accurate

I realize some bad habits

Still fall in the cracks of it

In remembrance of Dr. King

I too have a dream

Dreams of comfort ability

And what was once a prayer of hope

Has now become a present in reality

While my everlasting passion

For poetry over flows like a cup

Torn between two individuals

My style is original like my material

Who would even think

That on the 18th

A one of a kind Capricorn

Was born

Curtis Caliber Vanzant

Erotic Poetry…..

A Night of Many Nights

She calls me and tells me

That we need to talk

Now of course

I wondered about what

But those words

Was already surprising enough

Once we were both off work and

Me expecting to hear the rest of this

I guess

What she had in mind

Was more of a private conversation

See……..

We both spoke of body languages

Where

She became wet for me

And I became erect for her

Something nice and just right like

Me being polite by

Getting up

As she sits down

But that was just one of her

Positions

Of taking control of the situation

She even had a good head

On her shoulders as well

Bilingual by mixing it up

With a little

Oral presentations

I realized that

It was far from over

Curtis Caliber Vanzant

My turn bend over

She counter's by

Laying on her back

For me to explore her horizon

Inclined to tongue kiss

Both lips

Between when

The sunrises

And the sunsets

Because she meant

The world to me

That night I wanted her as wet

It Gets Deeper Than Potholes

As a doormat in the rain

And for me to be

As hard as a doorstopper

And playing no games

The chances of

One night stands

Was slim to none

A night of many nights

Because I believe in making her

Cum

A plethora of times

Curtis Caliber Vanzant

So

You can just leave

Your sexy outfit at the door

Because

At this point

I want to be all up in your business

Actually showing you

How much I miss you

Caressing you with the softest

It Gets Deeper Than Potholes

Kisses

That touches sensitive nerve

Endings

That registers

When it sends

Messages to your brain

Saying

Damn

With explanation points in all caps

At home

This is where

Our privatepartsmeet.com

While you be the magic

And I be the wand

Lets

Let's free our minds from any bad

Thoughts

Or whatever went wrong for today

By

Taking mental vacations

To wherever

It Gets Deeper Than Potholes

You would like…….

To go

Curtis Caliber Vanzant

Return to Sender

Besides the outfit that

Compliments the curves of her

Shape

Her smile was like

The icing on the cake

In which I couldn't help notice but

My primary focus wasn't based

On looks from the outside

I mean

It Gets Deeper Than Potholes

I was just curious enough

To want to get to know her
How she feels and
How she taste on the inside

Since it's up to the man
To approach then
You might as well say
I chose you
To come take this ride

Curtis Caliber Vanzant

Bless to be able to hold it down

Like a 9 to 5

And normally I don't

Kiss and tell

Or even describe how I might

Lick the stamp

Before I stick to the plan

But see

I rose to the occasion

Of my masculinity

For intimacy

To give you good

It Gets Deeper Than Potholes

D-fence tonight

And to taste your

Spirit and emotions like

Like it was some liquid erotic

Potion

While you open my

Tongue creates

Wave lengths in slow motion

Passionate bites to your pelvis so

I hope you not tickolious and

Curtis Caliber Vanzant

[Laughing]

Because of you

I just discovered

That peach cobbler is my favorite

So to take this even farther

I put my ear to it

To hear you cum twice

For starters so

I be damn if the phone rings

To disturb me and the

Moment between me and you

It Gets Deeper Than Potholes

And the sound that the

Vagina makes when I penetrate

With your sexy legs spreaded

In the degree of an

Obtuse angle because I want you

To remember

Who had the nerve?

To make you feel like this

And once you turn around

Applying the softest kisses

Curtis Caliber Vanzant

From your neck

Down to your spine

At the same time

You receiving this d***

Telling me how you want it and

How you may feel it

In your stomach but I'm

Just not ready to……………

Cummmmmm

Even with the magnum

I had to follow the rule of thumb or

One of the five keys and that's to

It Gets Deeper Than Potholes

Adjust to changing conditions

Which is

One of the reasons

Why I may arrive at my destination

Steady

But……….slow

Because it's so…. slippery when

It's wet

That's when I realized that

Behind closed doors

You turned me into a beast

And left your DNA

All over my clean sheets like

Perspiring pours

From your body

Searching for some type of relief

From me being

All up in your business………

Putting you into situations

That would have you sucking

Your middle finger

[Yes I said middle finger]

It Gets Deeper Than Potholes

In a fetal position

Creating my own version

Of different strokes

With continuous pokes

Because I can

So when we done

We gonna need this fan

To prevent overheating

Since we both seeking

Pleasure at its best

Then afterwards

We both laidback and cuddle

Curtis Caliber Vanzant

Like it's been awhile

Damn…………

It's kind of ironic

How this all started

From a beautiful smile

And a conversation

With the combination

Of a few things in common

But…………….

In order to receive this treatment

You may want to consider

To return to sender

So return to sender

It Gets Deeper Than Potholes
Vacationz

It's nothing wrong with

Taking vacations and

I am all for it

A chance to get away

From bull**** to daily agendas

And not to mention

A stress reliever

Just a

Temporary fix

Completely opposite

To something more permanent

Curtis Caliber Vanzant

Unless

Unless I was to move there

But unlike those vacations

This type was quite stimulating

See I wanted

I wanted

To visit her mind

Explore her body

And say hello to her soul

In that order

It Gets Deeper Than Potholes

That even the border line

That was the crevices

Had a glow

Although everything that glitters

Is not gold

She was like Paris to me

And my head was caught

In between that

London Bridge

Forgetting the disagreements

That was said

Curtis Caliber Vanzant

For her to remember

This particular king size bed

The land

The land was smooth and beautiful

My hands and lips

Caressed the curves and hips

Like footsteps upon hills

That led to the Zambezi River

Located in South Africa after

I French kissed her

It Gets Deeper Than Potholes

Tasting sweet

Like Georgia peaches

In which opened the doors to

Shaolin temple

And her Victoria's secret

The levees

The levees was like

The great walls of china

Of involuntary pelvic floor

Muscles

That constricted

Once I inserted my log in

Curtis Caliber Vanzant

For floatation

With a vulva as soft as pillows

No need for dildos

The sounds of a child stumping his

Feet

In small puddles

But she was no

Virgin Islands

I admit I did have

A couple of long islands

It Gets Deeper Than Potholes

And the excitement

Took us both on a Midwest flight

To the Caribbean's

I imagined

Sex on the beach

Just to reach the ultimate orgasm

That she seeks

Cause for that encounter

Representing all the way out of

Gary Indiana

It took long strokes

To please

So I was her the Indian giver

When she was in need

Giving and taking back

Multiple times until she climax

So I can actually see……

The outcome from my incoming

Of how she feels……..

It Gets Deeper Than Potholes

Egypt's valley of kings

Right in the middle of

Queensland in Australia

So when we get together

It's the battle of the sexes at last

Looking for that surrender flag

Now I know

I know what

They say about reading

But I remind you that this

Was also

Curtis Caliber Vanzant

Pleasurable and fundamental

And going

To these exotic places

Our body languages

Converse privately

But never silently in

More ways than one

I thought to myself

Damn

It Gets Deeper Than Potholes

I need another vacation

Curtis Caliber Vanzant

Bilingual Love

Ella era tan hermosa como esta pieza que
Escribió

She was just as beautiful

As this piece I wrote

The tangle of tongues

And taste buds that

Bi lingual love

Not knowing if I was her

Type of caliber

It Gets Deeper Than Potholes

I stayed in the background

Instead of chasing her

Silenzio……

Plus she

Might not want to be caught by me

But gradually we began to talk

In languages

Of verbal bondages

That astonishes the average

A work of art in the flesh

A human canvas

Better yet

A masterpiece

Since this is automatically put

In the category of

Erotic poetry

Then consider this a wordship

Fortunate to find and stimulate

At least eight thousands of the

Nerve endings

In her clitoris

I say this because

It Gets Deeper Than Potholes

She was all mines

Beyond a Valentine

Y una buena noche

This time

If love was illegal

Then we just committed a crime

Her smile and demeanor

Was the icing

On the cake

That included some

Tasty ingredients

She even had me speaking

In español like te quiero

After French kisses

That attempted to tie the knot

Between two different worlds

In which we came…….

To a mutual understanding

She was jazzy

And her dulcet moans

It Gets Deeper Than Potholes

Her moans sounded sexy

Like a saxophone

Je veins

I'm coming

I'm coming home

Where I lay right beside her

If my d***

Was still erect after sex

I would go deep

Just to sleep inside her

I was the provider

While she was a keeper

More than motivation

I compared her to meditation

As if

She was one of my seven chakras

We both liked old school impalas

And pasta

With no characteristics of an

Imposter

It Gets Deeper Than Potholes

Because we kept it real

With each other

Una relación recíproca

A reciprocal relationship

And it was just that

No wonder why they say

Two wrongs don't make a right

So for now…….

Curtis Caliber Vanzant

I think twice

It Gets Deeper Than Potholes

For The Streets…..

Curtis Caliber Vanzant

Broken Hearts

Sad to say but

A broken heart

Needs to be thrown in the garbage

Unless it can love again

Why walk around

Full of hate

So what it's a thin line

That don't mean you must cross it

Knowing there's no amendment

It Gets Deeper Than Potholes

For this

And the only one that comes close

Is the freedom of speech

No room for hatred in

This world

Whether it's another person's demeanor

Character, envy, jealousy, a bad past or Insecurities

And if so

Then it needs to be thrown in the garbage

Unless it can love again

Now talk about

Treating people the way

You would want to be treated

While some get defeated

By the cause of being mistreated

Like running out of love

With no care

Looking for company

To your misery

And if somebody ask

What do you gain

It Gets Deeper Than Potholes

You have no response

But instead you say f*** them all

Blaming others for your pain

And downfall

Yes

Broken hearts

The ones that don't smile at all

As if to be happy was a no no

With their middle fingers up

In all their photos

Curtis Caliber Vanzant

Society has shaped your mind

Into thinking that you

Have no reason to live

Looking sad and blue

When the truth is

You have every reason to

It's nothing wrong with

Falling in love

But remembering the feeling

Of heart break

It Gets Deeper Than Potholes

You stay here

Where you think

Is the safest place

And out of harm's way

Curtis Caliber Vanzant

My Thoughts

I once wondered that

For every life that is born into the

World

Does another one leave?

I started to roll up my sleeves

Just to try to write as many pieces

As my thoughts come to me

Like

Like unexpected visits

It Gets Deeper Than Potholes

That triggers my intellect and

Interpretation

Of what we and myself is facing

Because the pursuit of true

Happiness

Can sometimes be exhausting in

Chasing

In which no dollar can buy

So why try to adapt to the

Status quo when

Many believe

That your eyes

Are the windows to your soul

That is often exchanged

As collateral

And not to mention fame

Because if you a big time celebrity

It seems to me that

Your right to privacy gets revoked

Some may choke

And sum don't

While others may even give up

It Gets Deeper Than Potholes

And some won't

Whereas

The corner blocks

That auction off they product for

Profit

That becomes the hotspot

Thereafter

Then once you think about it

Your neighborhood drug dealer

Is no different from your average

Alcohol and tobacco manufacturer

Instead of just being

Supply and demand

You a dead man

If you f*** them over

Or a

Drug deal gone bad that

Ends up in blood shed

Like my older brother

Then there is a possibility

Of jail time

Which may seem fine for street cred

It Gets Deeper Than Potholes

But when it's all

Said and done

Being locked up

Ain't no fun son

I rather be a bird

So I can fly over bull****

And all the nonsense

That disturbs me with

No limits and no boundaries

To even stop me

I thought about that

When the question was asked to me

Knowing that

Confused minds

Can sometimes lead to casualties

But I guess it depends on your

Mentality

And on top of that

Thrown into a pot that's mixed

Like politics in a bag of tricks

It Gets Deeper Than Potholes

This stuff is fixed

Compared to events and

What you read in bible scripts

Because

Instead of being united as one

They use divide and conquer

Tactics

For sacred yet complicated

Mathematics so

Above it all

I began to look to the sky for

Curtis Caliber Vanzant

Answers

While sum in denial about

The wicked ways of the world as if

They only gained one opinion

Instead of three

About being diagnosed with cancer

And the stars that are revealed at

Night

See those stars

Look like peep holes

It Gets Deeper Than Potholes

So God and his angels can see

Just how long and strong one's

Faith can be

Because a wise man once told me

Despite of what goes wrong in

Your life

That even a broken clock

Can tell the right time

Twice

Curtis Caliber Vanzant

Moment of Silence

People be hollering

Stop the violence

But how many more black men

Women and children have to die

Before there is another moment of

Silence

Because that's easier said than

Done

While some using

It Gets Deeper Than Potholes

Human targets

And killing them off for some

Reason like

Like it's a killing season

Talking about respect and street

Credibility

Yelling they put in work

Living by that ol saying

That it's a thin line between

Love and hating

Listening to rap songs

Curtis Caliber Vanzant

From a few rap icons

It seems like

It's a thin line between

Promoting, provoking and

Educating

To confuse like

That's the solution

I call it talent abusing

Even in my hood of Gary, IN

You got to watch yourself

I remember

It Gets Deeper Than Potholes

Reading the paper about

A teenager shot and killed

An older man

Just because he blew his horn at

Him

For blocking a one way street

Our next door neighbors

Chicago being no different

Cause kids getting killed every

Weekend

By shootouts to stray bullets

That pierces the innocence

"Baby Thieves"

Taking and robbing lives

With non-remorseful eyes

You would think

With this type of mentality

Is just a phase

You think you gangsta

Cause you tote guns and

Shoot'em sideways

It Gets Deeper Than Potholes

Claiming you hard
Like you the only one
That got guns that spark

Hearing pistols popping
Bodies dropping not just in the
Dark

But it takes place
In broad daylight

While the population steady fall
It's like all we can do is hold

Curtis Caliber Vanzant

Neighborhood watches and rallies

At your local city hall

Only to give the impression like

We trying to solve them

Even got my latino hermanos y

Hermanas

Going through the same problem

Meanwhile some

Wishing for a way out

Like a genie trapped in a bottle

It Gets Deeper Than Potholes

Got pimps, dopeboys, OG's

And the bad guys in movies

Portrayed as your role models

Wanting a path to follow

So you figger

To name yourselves after

Mob figures

These wars over drugs,

Money, gangs and territory

Can sometimes lead up

To these incidents and

Curtis Caliber Vanzant

Any common sense

Would have seen it coming

What is the excuse?

"This is all I know"

Especially in the summer

I would love to see the day

When we

Rise above misleading

Propaganda

Senseless crimes

Among the ruthless

It Gets Deeper Than Potholes

From the east coast

To the west

And down south

Constantly being informed

By breaking news

Dressing up

Just to go to club and

Attending more funerals

Than church and job interviews

At the same time

Curtis Caliber Vanzant

I support and applaud

My black businesses but when

Shots reign out

You see everything

Plus the blood steins

But still no witnesses

Unless it was your kids

Sister, brother or relative

S***

Maybe even multiples of individuals

It Gets Deeper Than Potholes

Of all of the above

So to the community

Where is the love?

We say stop the violence

But in these streets

The question is

When will it cease

Instead of being deceased

And tell me

How many more men

Curtis Caliber Vanzant

Women and children

Got to die

Before there is another

Moment

Of silence

It Gets Deeper Than Potholes
Choices

See choices

Can be like mistakes

They can make or break you

While some may relate to

Impromptu judgment calls

Affect others like a ripple

And still

Before you've

Traded things for things

We all

Were given

Freewill

I believe part was

Destined to be

And the other half was up to you

Trying to distinguish

A curse from a blessing

Or a coincidence out the blue

What if unborn babies

Were given a choice too

It Gets Deeper Than Potholes

Knowing the world we live in

We call them miscarriages

A baby can be

Just as healthy as

Eating asparagus

But due to the mother's stress

Once developed at brain

Decided in the wound

To take its soul

And go back

To the one

Curtis Caliber Vanzant

Who created

Us

Yes

Unbelievable

Like the feelings

And personas of people

That tends to be completely fallible

And on the flipside

Left with no choice

Is how we felt inside

It Gets Deeper Than Potholes

Which explains why

People sacrifice

And do what they got to do just

To survive

From dropping out school

To joining the military

To obtaining GED's

High school diplomas

And pursuing college degrees

Or getting jobs

As a single parent

Just to make ends meet

Curtis Caliber Vanzant

To provide for your seeds

Even occupations to

Relations with

Individuals that may interest you

The choices

We make on a daily basis

Whether they altered by

Actions or persuasive voices

The decision

Is yours

Leaving the rest

Prone to being indecisive

Now that I have learned this

I must apply to my conscious

Because no matter what they say

About

Choosing your battles

Wisely

Curtis Caliber Vanzant

That sometimes God

Has chosen battles for you

To go through

Precisely

Content & Greed

I never was the flashy type

And I never lived a simple life

But contentment and greed

Draws a thin line

Between

What you want

And what you need

Now it may take a plethora of

Levels

To succeed

Unless money was inherited

Or working hard towards

Achievements

Minus government assistance

That others may depend on

No purpose

You just want it all

But I'm

Barely scraping the surface

Cause these issues can stretch

More than a mile

It Gets Deeper Than Potholes

And just maybe

Just maybe

Only change

The last person that read this

And to be honest

Being selfish

Can even be contagious

If you know what I mean

Or with the urge

To live above your means

To feel that satisfaction

And there goes

That thin line

That you may need a microscope

To see with

While on this side

You just blessed to still wake up

To see the sunrise

When you start to look at problems

As if they were nothing

But speed bumps on the road

It Gets Deeper Than Potholes

No soul sold

And the best thing to be

Is humble

Not disattached from emotion

You never know

This could be the one thing

That keeps this person going

And moving forward

With what life has to offer

But first

Unblocking all seven chakras

Or feeling like

You took a step

Ended up

Taking two backwards

Inside dying

But whoever said life

Will never be unfair and awkward

Was lying

And if you had nothing to loose

Then you

It Gets Deeper Than Potholes

Just might lose your cool

Add fuel to the fire

The hell with being patient

I rather

Turn it up

To get to

What I desire

At least before I retire

And there it goes again

Curtis Caliber Vanzant

Contentment and greed

That draws a thin line

Between what you want

And what you need

If you still lost

Then please refer to

A Poet's Peace

When I say

"That it cost to rich and it cost to

Be poor"

Cause once you open that door

To opportunity

You have a tendency to

Want more

Curtis Caliber Vanzant

I Am Cocaine

When abused I can turn families

Into miseries

I hit the black market in the 1960's

Known all over the world

For what I do

I am potent

And more powerful than you

It Gets Deeper Than Potholes

Through the streets and

Large bodies of water

Is how I get around

I can even turn a smile into a frown

Cocoa leaf Coca-Cola

I was the life of the party

And bought by high rollers

Making life just seem so unfair

Modifying dreams into nightmares

By being

Curtis Caliber Vanzant

Even more additive in my

Cheapest form

I turned loved ones into thieves

With women selling their bodies

Giving sexual favors over me

Weakness

And what's damn near

Down the drain

Is your career

S***

It Gets Deeper Than Potholes

Talk about rap icons

I even had the snowman

Talking about me

I was the s*** in movies

People didn't know what hit them

So to the dealers, let me work the block

You shall profit

Cause with my cliental

You probably won't even stop it

Curtis Caliber Vanzant

Misery is never alone

Even smoked by pregnant crack

Feins

Killing two birds with one stone

No hard work intended

Even though that's what they call me

I maybe white

But a racist

Is something that I am not

Only attracting people

It Gets Deeper Than Potholes

Who are just as vulnerable and

Materialistic as you

You recruit for me

And because of me

You kept them pleased

With money

But paranoid

Looking over your shoulder

Either for the cops

Or some fool

Trying to take what you got

Curtis Caliber Vanzant

It never stops

On the other hand

The feds giving fed time away

Like it was government cheese

Without them even

Looking at the mouse trap

With over pack prisons

I keep the system………

Flowing

And the only way out

Seek help, and higher power

It Gets Deeper Than Potholes

You need faith

Surrounded by positive people

Because I kill hope

My name is cocaine

And I put the D in dope

Curtis Caliber Vanzant

RBL

As a kid

I was blind at first

Until I sat down and

Did my homework

Reading between lines

Is when

I started to write lines

Instead of

Just being a target

It Gets Deeper Than Potholes

At the same time for some

They use to market

To mislead the rest

So who do you really impress

With your Malcom X

MLK pictures

Then demonstrate the opposite

Because you believe

Sagging is cool

Curtis Caliber Vanzant

You believe

Cash rules either

You not too clever or

Just a fool

Like the devil came to you

With his own proposition

Where ignorance ignores the rights

And listen to the wrongs

Do you even see the segregation?

In our own race

It Gets Deeper Than Potholes

Misery is never alone

So focused on playing pro ball

But with no education

Or any other skill

To fall back on

Not to mention

It's time to bring

And keep all our troops home

Contemplating on your next move

Wanting you to choose

Fighting over territory

Red and blues

No different from what

Political parties already do

Signing bills to

Execute a plan

Hoping

For a bipartisan decision

That's like asking

Rival gang members

It Gets Deeper Than Potholes

To shake hands

Think that's enough

What about the unfortunate

Before and after me

We probably would be

Amazed if we heard

Every homeless man's story

Prostitution

And dope feins

That can careless

About being clean

Or just

Curtis Caliber Vanzant

Can't kick the addiction

Self-destruction

For the few that's

Subjected to

Our own arousals and erections

For those who are

So sick of falling

In the ghetto

Forget selling dope

Because the Arabic's

It Gets Deeper Than Potholes

Are the real ones

That's balling

With their gas stations

And corner stores

The lack of training

To employ just as many people

As they say they

Put out jobs

Because college is not everything

And for damn show

Not for everyone

Curtis Caliber Vanzant

No offense to

Institutions

Because I been there

The commercials

Sounds promising

With a career once you graduate

Or job placement

Not a loss

More like another

Opportunity cost

See it's about

It Gets Deeper Than Potholes

What you can keep

Along with

What you got

Plus interest

Cash and credit

Because if you don't have it

Even when dating

Then you might as well forget it

Police brutality

Identity theft and scams

From imposters slash

Con artist slash

Opportunist

As technology grows

So does new ways to get over

Not paranoid though

And this piece

Was not

Meant to be controversial

Some of these issues

Goes beyond

A black and white thing

Mainly universal

Read the fine print

It's most likely

Used in contracts and documents

Why even question

My lyrical content

Struggle is necessary

According to statistics

Stress kills on a daily

Curtis Caliber Vanzant

So I write to relieve it

If you don't see the truth

Then one day

You shall see it

Reading between lines

A Second Chance

Why did he carry a gun?

His only intentions on using it

Was strictly for protection

It's kind of funny

Because that's exactly

What happened

It protected him

From one of man's greatest fears

Death

It rode with him to the end

His rodey, his little homie

The 380

Was his best friend

He was just trying to survive

Because he wasn't ready to die

He didn't have any kids

But understand, if he did

It Gets Deeper Than Potholes

He would like to see

What they could and would be

Unfortunately, to the judge

Self-defense wasn't

A good enough reason

For being guilty of this crime

They gave him 15 years

According to his background

Parole was a possibility

Hard time he was facing

He was patient

Curtis Caliber Vanzant

Playing ball, lifting weights

And he learned that reading

Really is fundamental

He got parole in 5

But the last four

No letters

A second chance was given

A new beginning

He has found new ways

Of dealing with morality

It Gets Deeper Than Potholes

So now he doesn't

Carry a gun

For protection

Instead he uses

His faith in Jesus Christ

And a cross as his weapon

Curtis Caliber Vanzant

Hard Time

I thought that I can control my own

Destiny

Destine to be

Something better than where I

Stand

But I can

With a plan to change

Yet I remain in the same place

Faced with vultures with

It Gets Deeper Than Potholes

Tattooed body sculptures

Hoping ta`

Wake up from this bad dream

Yet it seems as thou it's impossible

Especially for those who

Are on the outside

Looking in

But it's not

This is no lie, faith in God

And a little support from family

Alone

Is what keeps me alive

So you rise above all this

You can be locked up

But that doesn't mean

Your mind can't be free

To ignore the ignorance

So I challenge myself

Because it's too easy

To act crazy

It Gets Deeper Than Potholes

I try to stay humble

I must change

Better late than never

Whether you in that

Cell forever

Or whatever the case is

When it rains, it pours

Curtis Caliber Vanzant

And giving up is not in my

Vocabulary and neither

Should it be in yours

It Gets Deeper Than Potholes

RB2L

Well I guess I'm still a target

Once again

Not the one

They use to market

And part one issues

Still continues

While maintaining life's ups and

Downs

Like gas prices

This piece

I'm sure

Will remain universal

But will never make radio play

Even today with a cold beat

Under some cold sheets

Some folks remain sleep

Or just not listening

Using the oldest trick

In the book

By making you look

It Gets Deeper Than Potholes

With illusions, diversions and

Subliminal messages

For the mental

The real reason
Why he or she chose
To be with you

Tainted love

Manipulation versus
Discreet relations

Using sex just to be next

To move up

From being mediocre

Mixing business with pleasure

A favor for favor like

Publicity stunts

Bringing

Behind the scenes

To the fore front

For the public eye to see

It Gets Deeper Than Potholes

More drama

More dollars in reverse

Counter clockwise

My words……

If my words be

The death of me

Then there is no

Such thing

As a freedom of speech

The mystery of

Conspiracy theories

White collar crimes and

Greed

As if your name was

Charles Ponzi

With the majority

Wanting a piece of the pie

Even some nonprofit for profit

Organizations

It Gets Deeper Than Potholes

In which can't stop

For the sake of financial gain

Different faces

Different places

All playing

The same

Monopoly game

You want a dime

Well I want

To make change

Curtis Caliber Vanzant

To be able to

Shoot the truth off

From long range

To touch the lives

Of those that's not intimate

Painted pictures

Despite the judgment of

Artistic merit

Oblivious to the obvious

It Gets Deeper Than Potholes

Unless this time

You were actually reading

Between two lines

Curtis Caliber Vanzant

Steel City

We use to be the minority

In this city

That even brung foreigners

Together for work

Only 18 to 20 percent black

That gradually grew

To over 50 percent in them

1950's and 60's

After the layoffs in the mills

Segregation

It Gets Deeper Than Potholes

Political corruption

Then genocide

This is when I was born

So

You can find me

At the crossroads of Indiana

On them same streets

Named after them

Dead presidents

Although it's evident

That hope here

Is stagnant

Curtis Caliber Vanzant

Despite what some may say

Negative about my city

I have heard everything from

Murder capital

Ghost town

To gangsta island

One thing is for certain

Is that

We may multiply

But have done more subtracting

It Gets Deeper Than Potholes

Then adding

A place that

Had its heydays before

I was even thought of

Home of

The Jackson Five

And more

The King of pop

Where we pop

And drop off

No melting pot

This is not a tourist spot

Where the cost of living is a little

Cheaper

These are facts

Not counting

Two reasons

For high property tax

Like anywhere

You still just can't buy happiness

Just vacancies

It Gets Deeper Than Potholes

If you think business

See I love my city

How I use to love me

Some Archie Bees

In the 90's

On 11th Ave

With a population of less than

80,000 now

The other half

Is either dead

Incarcerated

Curtis Caliber Vanzant

Or moved away

Getting home sick

While some sit

Because they here

To stay

Like New Orleans

When Katrina hit

They said they not going

No where

It Gets Deeper Than Potholes

So they reside here

In my city

Steel City

Curtis Caliber Vanzant

Japanese Style…..

It Gets Deeper Than Potholes

Switch

The sun shines bright now

But the weather changes with

Personalities

Curtis Caliber Vanzant

Relations

The couple argues

Until they make love again

Temporary fix

What I See Here

Abandon buildings

Plenty of space everywhere

Hope is inside some

Curtis Caliber Vanzant

Road Trip

I captured the view

The ambiance of the land

The trees that responds

To the wind that turns windmills

That generates the power

It Gets Deeper Than Potholes

The Soft Side…..

Curtis Caliber Vanzant

Engram

First off

NO

I'm not the CEO

Of that publishing company

Named Ingram

And I'm not a poet

Even though

I was born during

National Poetry Month

On the 5th in 76

It Gets Deeper Than Potholes

But I still have a story

My story

Growing up

Without my parents

Faced with obstacles to cross

A female boss

You pass me by

Then you

Might as well say you loss

Curtis Caliber Vanzant

I got love to give

To my kids

And any man

Who accepts me

As a package deal

So excuse me

For my most

Inner thoughts

I'm just keeping it real

Because if you like this piece

Then automatically

It Gets Deeper Than Potholes

You like me

Better not be
For my hips and lips

Yawl men are a trip
Like tricks in a bag

The game I can spit back
Then ask you
How you feel about that?

See I rather play with words
And not hearts

Curtis Caliber Vanzant

They can be

Broken once opened

Because the whole time

You wore a mask

Only part time

This piece right here

Goes beyond rhymes

More like skin deep

Where spoken words

And the mind meets

By the way

I also teach

To all ages

Plus I don't live

Like Vegas

Counting numerous

Of occasions

Of being weak

Making sacrifices

Is what made me

The strongest

Sin City

Inhale the negativity

But you must exhale

Positive

To survive here

My temple

Shi City

It Gets Deeper Than Potholes

To All Females

An understandable cycle

In a female's life

On top of gender discrimination

The constant put downs

Of what you can't

And what man

Can do

Her story made proof

That shows

Curtis Caliber Vanzant

Beyond sex appeal

In all aspects of the word

You are beautiful

PERIOD…….

Abused But Not Destroyed

They say life is not fair
Better yet we all say that

But who especially the abused
Shall bare this pain
Who dares to put their hands
On someone as soft and beautiful
Besides a coward

That's like
That's like stepping on flowers

Curtis Caliber Vanzant

Replacing love for fears

Tears over happiness
While suffering for years
In domestic violence

That tends to keep most silent

Like that old snitch code
Which is easier said than done
To just go run and tell

But might make matters worse as
Well

See instead of loving you from the
Heart

In the minds of their victims
Is where they stem from

Intimidation is the game
To make inferior
Being superior is what they claim

Encouraging family and friends
That's concerned
Either close or distant

To stay out you'll business

But

I remember seeing her

Seeing that black eye covered by

Shades

Knowing it will fade

But the bruise in more internal

Creating low self-esteem

Exchanging dreams for nightmares

Of what he did

It Gets Deeper Than Potholes

With the possibility of misguided

Kids

See they were blessed with a set

A boy and a girl

And growing up

He thought to control

Was a must

And well she

She thought

The abuse was out of

Love

Curtis Caliber Vanzant

At one point existed but
Sad to see

Even the short distance
Between the fruits that fall from
The tree

Like a disease
This has come to be
A pandemic in communities

Because it's not just among urban
Families

It Gets Deeper Than Potholes

Politicians and their broken

Promises

That coincides with

Broken homes and

Broken hearts

In relationships

I know a few

Even Tupac asked

Can She Get Away?

For just an hour or two

So he gave

Curtis Caliber Vanzant

A list of demands saying

If he can't be with you

Then no one can

But I advise you to take a stand

And to never lose your dignity

Over no man

To fill a void

Because even though you were

Abused

It Gets Deeper Than Potholes

Whether it was mentally or

Physically

If you are reading this

Then obviously

You are not

Destroyed

Curtis Caliber Vanzant

Take Note

I'm cold

And I will continue

Writing until

The day

I freeze

Cutthroat

I shall bleed

Profusely

Poetry

www.ingramcontent.com/pod-product-compliance
Lightning Source LLC
Chambersburg PA
CBHW032145080426
42735CB00008B/595